THE ORDER OF MASS IN LATIN AND ENGLISH

CATHOLIC TRUTH SOCIETY
Publishers to the Holy See

ENGLISH TRANSLATION OF ORDER OF MASS
Approved by the Hierarchies of England & Wales
of Scotland and of Ireland.

Acknowledgment is due to the International Consultation on English Texts for translations of the Gloria, Nicene Creed, Dialogue before the Preface and Sanctus.

This text agrees with the original and is approved for use in Scotland, England & Wales and Ireland.

JOSEPH V. BOYD, *Secretary to the Liturgy Commission for Scotland.*
JOHN P. DEWIS, *on behalf of the Liturgy Commission for England & Wales*
PATRICK McGOLDRICK, *on behalf of the Irish Liturgical Commission.*

Imprimatur: Ralph R. Brown V.G.
Westminster 6th February, 1977

ORDO MISSAE
CUM POPULO

THE INTRODUCTORY RITES

The Mass may begin with the singing or recitation of the Entrance Antiphon *or a* Hymn *whilst the celebrant and servers approach the altar. The people stand.*

Celebrant: In nomine Patris, ✠ et Filii, et Spiritus Sancti.
People: **Amen.**

THE GREETING

One of the following greetings is used:

1. *C.* Gratia Domini nostri Iesu Christi, et caritas Dei, et communicatio Sancti Spiritus sit cum omnibus vobis.

   P. **Et cum spiritu tuo.**

---

2. *C.* Gratia vobis et pax a Deo Patre nostro et Domino Iesu Christo.
   P. **Benedictus Deus et Pater Domini nostri Iesu Christi.**
   Or: **Et cum spiritu tuo.**

---

3. *C.* Dominus vobiscum.
   P. **Et cum spiritu tuo.**

THE ORDER OF MASS
WITH A CONGREGATION

THE INTRODUCTORY RITES

The Mass may begin with the singing or recitation of the Entrance Antiphon *or a* Hymn *whilst the celebrant and servers approach the altar. The people stand.*

Celebrant: In the name of the Father, and of the Son, ✠ and of the Holy Spirit.
People: **Amen.**

THE GREETING

One of the following greetings is used:

1. *C.* The grace of our Lord Jesus Christ and the love of God
and the fellowship of the Holy Spirit be with you all.
P. **And also with you.**

---

2. *C.* The grace and peace of God our Father and the Lord Jesus Christ be with you.
P. **Blessed be God, the Father of our Lord Jesus Christ.**
Or: **And also with you.**

---

3. *C.* The Lord be with you.
P. **And also with you.**

THE PENITENTIAL RITE

The celebrant invites the people to repent of their sins using one of the following forms:

1. *C.* Fratres, agnoscamus peccata nostra, ut apti simus ad sacra mysteria celebranda.

After a brief silence all say:

Confiteor Deo omnipotenti et vobis,
fratres, quia peccavi nimis
cogitatione, verbo, opere et omissione:
(*all strike their breast*)
mea culpa, mea culpa, mea maxima culpa.
Ideo precor beatam Mariam semper Virginem;
omnes Angelos et Sanctos,
et vos, fratres, orare pro me
ad Dominum Deum nostrum.

---

2. *C.* Fratres, agnoscamus peccata nostra, ut apti simus ad sacra mysteria celebranda.

After a brief silence the celebrant continues:

Miserere nostri, Domine.

P. **Quia peccavimus tibi.**
C. Ostende nobis, Domine, misericordiam tuam.
P. **Et salutare tuum da nobis.**

---

3. *C.* Fratres, agnoscamus peccata nostra, ut apti simus ad sacra mysteria celebranda.

THE PENITENTIAL RITE

The celebrant invites the people to repent of their sins using one of the following forms:

1. *C.* My brothers and sisters (*or similar wording*), to prepare ourselves to celebrate the sacred mysteries, let us call to mind our sins.

After a brief silence all say:

I confess to almighty God,
and to you, my brothers and sisters,
that I have sinned
through my own fault (*all strike their breast*)
in my thoughts and in my words,
in what I have done,
and in what I have failed to do;
and I ask blessed Mary, ever virgin,
all the angels and saints,
and you, my brothers and sisters,
to pray for me to the Lord our God.

---

2. *C.* My brothers and sisters (*or similar wording*), to prepare ourselves to celebrate the sacred mysteries, let us call to mind our sins.

After a brief silence, the celebrant says:

Lord we have sinned against you : Lord, have mercy.

P. **Lord, have mercy.**
C. Lord, show us your mercy and love.
P. **And grant us your salvation.**

---

3. *C.* My brothers and sisters (*or similar wording*), to prepare ourselves to celebrate the sacred mysteries, let us call to mind our sins.

After a brief silence the celebrant says the following, or similar words. The people's response, however, remains the same.

Qui missus es sanare contritos corde : Kyrie, eleison.

P. **Kyrie, eleison.**
C. Qui peccatores vocare venisti : Christe, eleison.
P. **Christe, eleison.**
C. Qui ad dexteram Patris sedes, ad interpellandum pro nobis : Kyrie, eleison.
P. **Kyrie, eleison.**

The Act of Penance *is followed by the* Absolution.

C. Misereatur nostri omnipotens Deus
et, dimissis peccatis nostris,
perducat nos ad vitam æternam.
P. **Amen.**

The Kyrie eleison *now follows unless it has already been used in one of the forms of the* Act of Penance.

C. Kyrie, eleison.
P. **Kyrie, eleison.**
C. Christe, eleison.
P. **Christe, eleison.**
C. Kyrie, eleison.
P. **Kyrie, eleison.**

After a brief silence the celebrant says the following, or similar words. The people's response, however, remains the same.

You were sent to heal the contrite:
Lord, have mercy.

P. **Lord, have mercy.**

C. You came to call sinners:
Christ, have mercy.

P. **Christ, have mercy.**

C. You plead for us at the right hand of the Father:
Lord, have mercy.

P. **Lord, have mercy.**

The Act of Penance *is followed by the* Absolution.

C. May almighty God have mercy on us,
forgive us our sins,
and bring us to everlasting life.

P. **Amen.**

The Kyrie eleison *now follows unless it has already been used in one of the forms of the* Act of Penance.

C. Lord, have mercy.

P. **Lord, have mercy.**

C. Christ, have mercy.

P. **Christ, have mercy.**

C. Lord, have mercy.

P. **Lord, have mercy.**

THE GLORIA

If it is to be said, the Gloria *now follows:*
Gloria in excelsis Deo
et in terra pax hominibus bonæ voluntatis.
Laudamus te,
benedicimus te,
adoramus te,
glorificamus te,
gratias agimus tibi propter magnam gloriam tuam,
Domine Deus, Rex cælestis,
Deus Pater omnipotens.
Domine Fili unigenite, Iesu Christe,
Domine Deus, Agnus Dei, Filius Patris,
qui tollis peccata mundi, miserere nobis;
qui tollis peccata mundi, suscipe deprecationem nostram.
Qui sedes ad dexteram Patris, miserere nobis.
Quoniam tu solus Sanctus, tu solus Dominus, tu solus Altissimus,
Jesu Christe, cum Sancto Spiritu: in gloria Dei Patris. Amen.

The priest collects the prayerful thoughts of everyone present.
C. Oremus.

At the end of the Collect:
P. **Amen.**

THE GLORIA

If it is to be said, the Gloria *now follows:*

Glory to God in the highest,
and peace to his people on earth.

Lord God, heavenly King,
almighty God and Father,
we worship you, we give you thanks,
we praise you for your glory.

Lord Jesus Christ, only Son of the Father,
Lord God, Lamb of God,
you take away the sin of the world:
have mercy on us;
you are seated at the right hand of the Father:
receive our prayer.

For you alone are the Holy One,
you alone are the Lord,
you alone are the Most High,
Jesus Christ,
with the Holy Spirit,
in the glory of God the Father. Amen.

The priest collects the prayerful thoughts of everyone present.
C. Let us pray.

At the end of the Collect:
P. **Amen.**

THE LITURGY OF THE WORD

The Liturgy of the Word *is generally in the language of the people, except that the* responsorial psalm *may be sung in Latin.*

At international congresses it may be preferable to use Latin rather than the local language, as follows:
At the end of the Reading :
Verbum Domini.
The people reply:
Deo gratias.
Before the Gospel :
C. Dominus vobiscum.
P. **Et cum spiritu tuo.**
C. Lectio sancti Evangelii secundum *N.*
P. **Gloria tibi, Domine.**
At the end of the Gospel :
C. Verbum Domini.
P. **Laus tibi, Christe.**

THE PROFESSION OF FAITH

If it is to be said, the Creed *now follows:*
Credo in unum Deum,
Patrem omnipotentem, factorem cæli et terræ,
visibilium omnium et invisibilium.

Et in unum Dominum Iesum Christum,
Filium Dei unigenitum,
et ex Patre natum ante omnia sæcula.
Deum de Deo, lumen de lumine, Deum verum de Deo vero,

THE LITURGY OF THE WORD

At the end of each Reading *the Lector says:*
This is the word of the Lord.

P. **Thanks be to God.**
Before reading the Gospel, *the celebrant greets the people:*
The Lord be with you.
P. **And also with you.**
He then announces the Gospel from which the Reading *is chosen. The people reply:*
Glory to you, Lord.

At the end of the Gospel, *the priest announces:*
This is the Gospel of the Lord.
P. **Praise to you, Lord Jesus Christ.**

THE PROFESSION OF FAITH

If it is to be said, the Creed *now follows:*
We believe in one God,
the Father, the Almighty,
maker of heaven and earth,
of all that is, seen and unseen.

We believe in one Lord, Jesus Christ,
the only Son of God,
eternally begotten of the Father,
God from God, Light from Light,
true God from true God,

genitum, non factum, consubstantialem Patri:
per quem omnia facta sunt.
Qui propter nos homines et propter nostram salutem descendit de cælis.
Et incarnatus est de Spiritu Sancto
ex Maria Virgine, et homo factus est.
Crucifixus etiam pro nobis sub Pontio Pilato;
passus et sepultus est,
et resurrexit tertia die, secundum Scripturas,
et ascendit in cælum, sedet ad dexteram Patris.
Et iterum venturus est cum gloria, iudicare vivos et mortuos,
cuius regni non erit finis.

Et in Spiritum Sanctum, Dominum et vivificantem:
qui ex Patre Filioque procedit.
Qui cum Patre et Filio simul adoratur et conglorificatur:
qui locutus est per prophetas.
Et unam, sanctam, catholicam et apostolicam Ecclesiam.
Confiteor unum baptisma in remissionem peccatorum.
Et exspecto resurrectionem mortuorum,
et vitam venturi sæculi. Amen.

The Bidding Prayer *or* Prayer of the Faithful *now follows.*

begotten, not made,
of one Being with the Father.
Through him all things were made.
For us men and for our salvation
he came down from heaven:
by the power of the Holy Spirit
he became incarnate from the Virgin Mary,
and was made man. (*All bow.*)
For our sake he was crucified under Pontius Pilate; he suffered death and was buried.
On the third day he rose again
in accordance with the Scriptures;
he ascended into heaven
and is seated at the right hand of the Father.
He will come again in glory to judge the living and the dead,
and his kingdom will have no end.

We believe in the Holy Spirit, the Lord, the giver of life,
who proceeds from the Father and the Son.
With the Father and the Son he is worshipped and glorified.
He has spoken through the Prophets.
We believe in one holy catholic and apostolic Church.
We acknowledge one baptism for the forgiveness of sins.
We look for the resurrection of the dead,
and the life of the world to come. Amen.

The Bidding Prayer *or* Prayer of the Faithful *now follows*

THE LITURGY OF THE EUCHARIST

THE PREPARATION OF THE GIFTS

A song, chant, anthem or other suitable hymn may be sung as the gifts are brought to the altar. If there is no antiphon or hymn, the celebrant may say the following prayers in an audible voice.

C. Benedictus es, Domine, Deus universi,
quia de tua largitate accepimus panem,
quem tibi offerimus,
fructum terræ et operis manuum hominum,
ex quo nobis fiet panis vitæ.

P. **Benedictus Deus in sæcula.**

(*Omitted if singing is in progress.*)

C. Benedictus es, Domine, Deus universi,
quia de tua largitate accepimus vinum,
quod tibi offerimus,
fructum vitis et operis manuum hominum,
ex quo nobis fiet potus spiritalis.

P. **Benedictus Deus in sæcula.**

(*Omitted if singing is in progress.*)

After washing his hands the celebrant says:

Orate, fratres:
ut meum ac vestrum sacrificium
acceptabile fiat apud Deum Patrem omnipotentem.

P. **Suscipiat Dominus sacrificium de manibus tuis
ad laudem et gloriam nominis sui,
ad utilitatem quoque nostram
totiusque Ecclesiæ suæ sanctæ.**

The celebrant then reads the Prayer over the Gifts, *at the end of which:*

P. **Amen.**

THE LITURGY OF THE EUCHARIST

THE PREPARATION OF THE GIFTS

A song, chant, anthem or other suitable hymn may be sung as the gifts are brought to the altar. If there is no antiphon or hymn, the celebrant may say the following prayers in an audible voice.

C. Blessed are you, Lord, God of all creation.
Through your goodness we have this bread to offer,
which earth has given and human hands have made.
It will become for us the bread of life.

P. **Blessed be God for ever.** (*Omitted if singing is in progress.*)

C. Blessed are you, Lord, God of all creation.
Through your goodness we have this wine to offer,
fruit of the vine and work of human hands.
It will become our spiritual drink.

P. **Blessed be God for ever.** (*Omitted if singing is in progress.*)

After washing his hands the celebrant says:
Pray, brethren, that my sacrifice and yours
[*In Ireland,* ' . . . that our sacrifice']
may be acceptable to God, the almighty Father.

P. **May the Lord accept the sacrifice at your hands**
for the praise and glory of his name,
for our good, and the good of all his Church.

The celebrant then reads the Prayer over the Gifts, *at the end of which:*

P. **Amen.**

THE EUCHARISTIC PRAYER

C. Dominus vobiscum.
P. **Et cum spiritu tuo.**
C. Sursum corda.
P. **Habemus ad Dominum.**
C. Gratias agamus Domino Deo nostro.
P. **Dignum et iustum est.**

The celebrant then reads the Preface, *at the end of which the people join with him saying:*
Sanctus, Sanctus, Sanctus Dominus Deus Sabaoth.
Pleni sunt cæli et terra gloria tua.
Hosanna in excelsis.
Benedictus qui venit in nomine Domini.
Hosanna in excelsis.

The Eucharistic Prayer of praise and thanksgiving is the centre and high point of the whole celebration. The congregation joins Christ in acknowledging the works of God and in offering his sacrifice to the Father. It takes one of the following forms. (*The celebrant may omit what is in brackets.*)

Eucharistic Prayer I

Te igitur, clementissime Pater,
per Iesum Christum, Filium tuum, Dominum nostrum,
supplices rogamus ac petimus,
uti accepta habeas
et benedicas ✠ hæc dona, hæc munera,
hæc sancta sacrificia illibata,
in primis, quæ tibi offerimus
pro Ecclesia tua sancta catholica:
quam pacificare, custodire, adunare
et regere digneris toto orbe terrarum:

THE EUCHARISTIC PRAYER

C. The Lord be with you.
P. **And also with you.**
C. Lift up your hearts.
P. **We lift them up to the Lord.**
C. Let us give thanks to the Lord our God.
P. **It is right to give him thanks and praise.**

The celebrant then reads the Preface, *at the end of which the People join with him saying:*
Holy, holy, holy Lord, God of power and might,
heaven and earth are full of your glory.
Hosanna in the highest.
Blessed is he who comes in the name of the Lord.
Hosanna in the highest.

The Eucharistic Prayer of praise and thanksgiving is the centre and high point of the whole celebration. The congregation joins Christ in acknowledging the works of God and in offering his sacrifice to the Father. It takes one of the following forms. (*The celebrant may omit what is in brackets.*)

Eucharistic Prayer I

We come to you, Father,
with praise and thanksgiving,
through Jesus Christ your Son.
Through him we ask you to accept and bless ✠
these gifts we offer you in sacrifice.
We offer them for your holy catholic Church,
watch over it, Lord, and guide it;
grant it peace and unity throughout the world.

una cum famulo tuo Papa nostro *N.*
et Antistite nostro *N.*
et omnibus orthodoxis atque catholicæ et apostolicæ
fidei cultoribus.

Memento, Domine, famulorum famularumque tuarum
N. and *N.*
et omnium circumstantium,
quorum tibi fides cognita est et nota devotio,
pro quibus tibi offerimus:
vel qui tibi offerunt hoc sacrificium laudis,
pro se suisque omnibus:
pro redemptione animarum suarum,
pre spe salutis et incolumitatis suæ:
tibique reddunt vota sua
æterno Deo, vivo et vero.

Communicantes,
et memoriam venerantes,
in primis gloriosæ semper Virginis Mariæ,
Genetricis Dei et Domini nostri Iesu Christi:
sed et beati Ioseph, eiusdem Virginis Sponsi,
et beatorum Apostolorum ac Martyrum tuorum,
Petri et Pauli, Andreæ,
(Iacobi, Ioannis,
Thomae, Iacobi, Philippi,
Bartholomæi, Matthæi,
Simonis et Thaddæi:
Lini, Cleti, Clementis, Xysti,
Cornelii, Cypriani,
Laurentii, Chrysogoni,
Ioannis et Pauli,
Cosmæ et Damiani)
et omnium Sanctorum tuorum;
quorum meritis precibusque concedas,

We offer them for *N.* our Pope,
for *N.* our bishop,
and for all who hold and teach the catholic faith
that comes to us from the apostles.

Remember, Lord, your people,
especially those for whom we now pray, *N.* and *N.*
Remember all of us gathered here before you.
You know how firmly we believe in you
and dedicate ourselves to you.
We offer you this sacrifice of praise
for ourselves and those who are dear to us.
We pray to you, our living and true God,
for our well-being and redemption.

In union with the whole Church
we honour Mary,
the ever-virgin mother of Jesus Christ our Lord and God.
We honour Joseph, her husband,
the apostles and martyrs
Peter and Paul, Andrew,
(James, John, Thomas,
James, Philip,
Bartholomew, Matthew, Simon and Jude;
we honour Linus, Cletus, Clement, Sixtus,
Cornelius, Cyprian, Lawrence, Chrysogonus,
John and Paul, Cosmas and Damian)
and all the saints.

May their merits and prayers
gain us your constant help and protection.
(Through Christ our Lord. Amen.)

ut in omnibus protectionis tuæ muniamur auxilio.
(Per Christum Dominum nostrum. Amen.)

Hanc igitur oblationem servitutis nostræ,
sed et cunctæ familiæ tuæ,
quæsumus, Domine, ut placatus accipias:
diesque nostros in tua pace disponas,
atque ab æterna damnatione nos eripi
et in electorum tuorum iubeas grege numerari.
(Per Christum Dominum nostrum. Amen.)

Quam oblationem tu, Deus, in omnibus, quæsumus,
benedictam, adscriptam, ratam,
rationabilem, acceptabilemque facere digneris:
ut nobis Corpus et Sanguis fiat dilectissimi Filii tui,
Domini nostri Iesu Christi.

Qui, pridie quam pateretur,
accepit panem in sanctas ac venerabiles manus suas,
et elevatis oculis in cælum
ad te Deum Patrem suum omnipotentem,
tibi gratias agens benedixit,
fregit,
deditque discipulis suis, dicens:

Accipite et manducate ex hoc omnes:
hoc est enim Corpus meum,
quod pro vobis tradetur.

Father, accept this offering
from your whole family.
Grant us your peace in this life,
save us from final damnation,
and count us among those you have chosen.

(Through Christ our Lord. Amen.)

Bless and approve our offering;
make it acceptable to you,
an offering in spirit and in truth.
Let it become for us
the body and blood of Jesus Christ,
your only Son, our Lord.

The day before he suffered
he took bread in his sacred hands
and looking up to heaven,
to you, his almighty Father,
he gave you thanks and praise.
He broke the bread
gave it to his disciples, and said:

Take this, all of you, and eat it:
this is my body which will be given up for you.

Simili modo, postquam cenatum est,
accipiens et hunc præclarum calicem
in sanctas ac venerabiles manus suas,
item tibi gratias agens benedixit,
deditque discipulis suis, dicens;

Accipite et bibite ex eo omnes:
hic est enim calix Sanguinis mei,
novi et æterni testamenti,
qui pro vobis et pro multis effundetur
in remissionem peccatorum.

Hoc facite in meam commemorationem.

Mysterium fidei.

The people reply using one of these acclamations:

1. **Mortem tuam annuntiamus, Domine,
et tuam resurrectionem confitemur, donec
venias.**

2. **Quotiescumque manducamus panem hunc
et calicem bibimus,
mortem tuam annuntiamus, Domine, donec
venias.**

3. **Salvator mundi, salva nos,
qui per crucem et resurrectionem tuam
liberasti nos.**

When supper was ended,
he took the cup.
Again he gave you thanks and praise,
gave the cup to his disciples, and said :

Take this, all of you, and drink from it:
this is the cup of my blood,
the blood of the new and everlasting covenant.
It will be shed for you and for all men
so that sins may be forgiven.

Do this in memory of me.

Let us proclaim the mystery of faith :

The people reply using one of these acclamations:

1. **Christ has died,**
   Christ is risen,
   Christ will come again.

2. **Dying you destroyed our death,**
   rising you restored our life.
   Lord Jesus, come in glory.

3. **When we eat this bread and drink this cup,**
   we proclaim your death, Lord Jesus,
   until you come in glory.

4. **Lord, by your cross and resurrection**
   you have set us free.
   You are the Saviour of the world.

The celebrant continues:
Unde et memores, Domine,
nos servi tui,
sed et plebs tua sancta,
eiusdem Christi, Filii tui, Domini nostri,
tam beatæ passionis,
necnon et ab inferis resurrectionis,
sed et in cælos gloriosæ ascensionis :
offerimus præclaræ maiestati tuæ
de tuis donis ac datis
hostiam puram,
hostiam sanctam,
hostiam immaculatam,
Panem sanctum vitæ æternæ
et Calicem salutis perpetuæ.

Supra quæ propitio ac sereno vultu
respicere digneris :
et accepta habere,
sicuti accepta habere dignatus es
munera pueri tui iusti Abel,
et sacrificium Patriarchæ nostri Abrahæ,
et quod tibi obtulit summus sacerdos tuus
Melchisedech,
sanctum sacrificium, immaculatam hostiam.

Supplices te rogamus, omnipotens Deus :
iube hæc perferri per manus sancti Angeli tui
in sublime altare tuum,
in conspectu divinæ maiestatis tuæ ;
ut, quotquot ex hac altaris participatione
sacrosanctum Filii tui Corpus et Sanguinem
sumpserimus,
omni benedictione cælesti et gratia repleamur.
(Per Christum Dominum nostrum. Amen.)

The celebrant continues:
Father, we celebrate the memory of Christ, your Son.
We, your people and your ministers,
recall his passion,
his resurrection from the dead,
and his ascension into glory;
and from the many gifts you have given us
we offer to you, God of glory and majesty,
this holy and perfect sacrifice:
the bread of life
and the cup of eternal salvation.
Look with favour on these offerings
and accept them as once you accepted
the gifts of your servant Abel,
the sacrifice of Abraham, our father in faith,
and the bread and wine offered by your priest
Melchisedech.

Almighty God,
we pray that your angel may take this sacrifice
to your altar in heaven.
Then, as we receive from this altar
the sacred body and blood of your Son,
let us be filled with every grace and blessing.
(Through Christ our Lord. Amen.)

Memento etiam, Domine, famulorum famularumque
tuarum *N.* et *N.*,
qui nos præcesserunt cum signo fidei,
et dormiunt in somno pacis.
Ipsis, Domine, et omnibus in Christo quiescentibus,
locum refrigerii, lucis et pacis,
ut indulgeas deprecamur.
(Per Christum Dominum nostrum. Amen.)

Nobis quoque peccatoribus famulis tuis,
de multitudine miserationum tuarum sperantibus,
partem aliquam et societatem donare digneris
cum tuis sanctis Apostolis et Martyribus :
cum Ioanne, Stephano,
Matthia, Barnaba,
(Ignatio, Alexandro,
Marcellino, Petro,
Felicitate, Perpetua,
Agatha, Lucia,
Agnete, Cæcilia, Anastasia)
et omnibus Sanctis tuis :
intra quorum nos consortium,
non æstimator meriti, sed veniæ,
quæsumus, largitor admitte.

Per Christum Dominum nostrum,
per quem hæc omnia, Domine,
semper bona creas, sanctificas, vivificas, benedicis,
et præstas nobis.

Per ipsum, et cum ipso, et in ipso,
est tibi Deo Patri omnipotenti,
in unitate Spiritus Sancti,
omnis honor et gloria
per omnia sæcula sæculorum.

P. **Amen.**

Remember, Lord, those who have died
and have gone before us marked with the sign of faith,
especially those for whom we now pray, *N.* and *N.*
May these, and all who sleep in Christ,
find in your presence
light, happiness, and peace.
(Through Christ our Lord. Amen.)

For ourselves, too, we ask
some share in the fellowship of your apostles and
martyrs,
with John the Baptist, Stephen, Matthias, Barnabas,
(Ignatius, Alexander, Marcellinus, Peter,
Felicity, Perpetua, Agatha, Lucy,
Agnes, Cecilia, Anastasia)
and all the saints.

Though we are sinners,
we trust in your mercy and love.
Do not consider what we truly deserve,
but grant us your forgiveness.

Through Christ our Lord
you give us all these gifts.
You fill them with life and goodness,
you bless them and make them holy.

Through him, with him, in him,
in the unity of the Holy Spirit,
all glory and honour is yours,
almighty Father,
for ever and ever.

P. **Amen.**

Eucharistic Prayer II

Vere Sanctus es, Domine, fons omnis sanctitatis.
Hæc ergo dona, quæsumus,
Spiritus tui rore sanctifica,
ut nobis Corpus et ✠ Sanguis fiant
Domini nostri Iesu Christi.

Qui cum Passioni voluntarie traderetur,
accepit panem et gratias agens fregit,
deditque discipulis suis, dicens :

Accipite et manducate ex hoc omnes :
hoc est enim Corpus meum,
quod pro vobis tradetur.

Simili modo, postquam cenatum est,
accipiens et calicem,
iterum gratias agens dedit discipulis suis, dicens :

Accipite et bibite ex eo omnes :
hic est enim calix Sanguinis mei
novi et æterni testamenti,
qui pro vobis et pro multis effundetur
in remissionem peccatorum.

Hoc facite in meam commemorationem.

Mysterium fidei :

Eucharistic Prayer II

Lord you are holy indeed,
the fountain of all holiness.
Let your Spirit come upon these gifts to make them holy
so that they may become for us
the body ✠ and blood of our Lord, Jesus Christ.

Before he was given up to death,
a death he freely accepted,
he took bread and gave you thanks.
He broke the bread,
gave it to his disciples, and said :

Take this, all of you, and eat it:
this is my body which will be given up for you.

When supper was ended, he took the cup.
Again he gave you thanks and praise,
gave the cup to his disciples, and said :

Take this, all of you, and drink from it:
this is the cup of my blood,
the blood of the new and everlasting covenant.
It will be shed for you and for all men
so that sins may be forgiven.
Do this in memory of me.

Let us proclaim the mystery of faith :

The people reply using one of these acclamations:

1. **Mortem tuam annuntiamus, Domine,
et tuam resurrectionem confitemur, donec
venias.**

2. **Quotiescumque manducamus panem hunc
et calicem bibimus,
mortem tuam annuntiamus, Domine, donec
venias.**

3. **Salvator mundi, salva nos,
qui per crucem et resurrectionem tuam
liberasti nos.**

Memores igitur mortis et resurrectionis eius,
tibi, Domine, panem vitæ
et calicem salutis offerimus,
gratias agentes quia nos dignos habuisti
astare coram te et tibi ministrare.

Et supplices deprecamur
ut Corporis et Sanguinis Christi participes
a Spiritu Sancto congregemur in unum.

Recordare, Domine, Ecclesiæ tuæ toto orbe diffusæ,
ut eam in caritate perficias
una cum Papa nostro *N.* et Episcopo nostro *N.*
et universo clero.

In Masses for the Dead *the following may be added:*
Memento famuli tui (famulæ tuæ) *N.*,
quem (quam) (hodie) ad te ex hoc mundo vocasti.
Concede, ut, qui (quæ) complantatus (complantata)
fuit similitudini mortis Filii tui,
simul fiat et resurrectionis ipsius.

The people reply using one of these acclamations:

1. **Christ has died,**
   Christ is risen,
   Christ will come again.

2. **Dying you destroyed our death,**
   rising you restored our life.
   Lord Jesus, come in glory.

3. **When we eat this bread and drink this cup,**
   we proclaim your death, Lord Jesus,
   until you come in glory.

4. **Lord, by your cross and resurrection**
   you have set us free.
   You are the Saviour of the world.

In memory of his death and resurrection,
we offer you, Father, this life-giving bread,
this saving cup.
We thank you for counting us worthy
to stand in your presence and serve you.
May all of us who share in the body and blood of Christ
be brought together in unity by the Holy Spirit.

Lord, remember your Church throughout the world;
make us grow in love,
together with *N.* our Pope,
N. our bishop, and all the clergy.

In Masses for the Dead *the following may be added:*
Remember *N.*, whom you have called from this life.
In baptism he/she died with Christ:
may he/she also share his resurrection.

Memento etiam fratrum nostrorum,
qui in spe resurrectionis dormierunt,
omniumque in tua miseratione defunctorum,
et eos in lumen vultus tui admitte.
Omnium nostrum, quæsumus, miserere,
ut cum beata Dei Genetrice Virgine Maria,
beatis Apostolis et omnibus Sanctis,
qui tibi a sæculo placuerunt,
æternæ vitæ mereamur esse consortes,
et te laudemus et glorificemus
per Filium tuum Iesum Christum.

Per ipsum, et cum ipso, et in ipso,
est tibi Deo Patri omnipotenti,
in unitate Spiritus Sancti,
omnis honor et gloria
per omnia sæcula sæculorum.

P. **Amen.**

Remember our brothers and sisters
who have gone to their rest
in the hope of rising again;
bring them and all the departed
into the light of your presence.
Have mercy on us all;
make us worthy to share eternal life
with Mary, the virgin mother of God,
with the apostles,
and with all the saints who have done your will
throughout the ages.
May we praise you in union with them,
and give you glory
through your Son, Jesus Christ.

Through him, with him, in him,
in the unity of the Holy Spirit,
all glory and honour is yours,
almighty Father
for ever and ever.

P. **Amen.**

Eucharistic Prayer III

Vere Sanctus es, Domine,
et merito te laudat omnis a te condita creatura,
quia per Filium tuum,
Dominum nostrum Iesum Christum,
Spiritus Sancti operante virtute,
vivificas et sanctificas universa,
et populum tibi congregare non desinis,
ut a solis ortu usque ad occasum
oblatio munda offeratur nomini tuo.

Supplices ergo te, Domine, deprecamur,
ut hæc munera, quæ tibi sacranda detulimus,
eodem Spiritu sanctificare digneris,
ut Corpus et ✠ Sanguis fiant
Filii tui Domini nostri Iesu Christi,
cuius mandato hæc mysteria celebramus.

Ipse enim in qua nocte tradebatur
accepit panem
et tibi gratias agens benedixit,
fregit, deditque discipulis suis, dicens :

Accipite et manducate ex hoc omnes :
hoc est enim Corpus meum,
quod pro vobis tradetur.

Simili modo, postquam cenatum est,
accipiens calicem,
et tibi gratias agens benedixit,
deditque discipulis suis, dicens :

Eucharistic Prayer III

Father, you are holy indeed,
and all creation rightly gives you praise.
All life, all holiness comes from you
through your Son, Jesus Christ our Lord,
by the working of the Holy Spirit.
From age to age you gather a people to yourself,
so that from east to west
a perfect offering may be made
to the glory of your name.

And so, Father, we bring you these gifts.
We ask you to make them holy by the power of your
Spirit,
that they may become the body ✠ and blood
of your Son, our Lord Jesus Christ,
at whose command we celebrate this eucharist.

On the night he was betrayed,
he took bread and gave you thanks and praise.
He broke the bread, gave it to his disciples, and said:

Take this, all of you, and eat it:
this is my body which will be given up for
you.

When supper was ended, he took the cup.
Again he gave you thanks and praise,
gave the cup to his disciples, and said:

Accipite et bibite ex eo omnes:
hic est enim calix Sanguinis mei
novi et æterni testamenti,
qui pro vobis et pro multis effundetur
in remissionem peccatorum.

Hoc facite in meam commemorationem.

Mysterium fidei:

The people reply using one of these acclamations:

1. **Mortem tuam annuntiamus, Domine, et tuam resurrectionem confitemur, donec venias.**

2. **Quotiescumque manducamus panem hunc et calicem bibimus, mortem tuam annuntiamus, Domine, donec venias.**

3. **Salvator mundi, salva nos, qui per crucem et resurrectionem tuam liberasti nos.**

Memores igitur, Domine,
eiusdem Filii tui salutiferæ passionis
necnon mirabilis resurrectionis
et ascensionis in cælum,
sed et præstolantes alterum eius adventum,
offerimus tibi. gratias referentes,
hoc sacrificium vivum et sanctum.

Take this, all of you, and drink from it:
this is the cup of my blood,
the blood of the new and everlasting convenant.
It will be shed for you and for all men
so that sins may be forgiven.
Do this in memory of me.

Let us proclaim the mystery of faith:

The people reply using one of these acclamations:

1. **Christ has died,
   Christ is risen,
   Christ will come again.**

2. **Dying you destroyed our death,
   rising you restored our life.
   Lord Jesus, come in glory.**

3. **When we eat this bread and drink this cup,
   we proclaim your death, Lord Jesus,
   until you come in glory.**

4. **Lord, by your cross and resurrection
   you have set us free.
   You are the Saviour of the world.**

Father, calling to mind the death your Son endured for our salvation,
his glorious resurrection and ascension into heaven,
and ready to greet him when he comes again,
we offer you in thanksgiving this holy and living sacrifice.

Respice, quæsumus, in oblationem Ecclesiæ tuæ
et, agnoscens Hostiam,
cuius voluisti immolatione placari,
concede, ut qui Corpore et Sanguine Filii tui reficimur,
Spiritu eius Sancto repleti,
unum corpus et unus spiritus inveniamur in Christo.

Ipse nos tibi perficiat munus æternum,
ut cum electis tuis hereditatem consequi valeamus,
in primis cum beatissima Virgine, Dei Genetrice, Maria,
cum beatis Apostolis tuis et gloriosis Martyribus
(cum Sancto *N., the saint of the day or the patron saint*)
et omnibus Sanctis,
quorum intercessione
perpetuo apud te confidimus adiuvari.

Hæc Hostia nostræ reconciliationis proficiat,
quæsumus, Domine,
ad totius mundi pacem atque salutem.
Ecclesiam tuam, peregrinantem in terra,
in fide et caritate firmare digneris
cum famulo tuo Papa nostro *N.* et Episcopo nostro *N.*
cum episcopali ordine et universo clero
et omni populo acquisitionis tuæ.
Votis huius familiæ, quam tibi astare voluisti,
adesto propitius.
Omnes filios tuos ubique dispersos
tibi, clemens Pater, miseratus coniunge.

Look with favour on your Church's offering,
and see the Victim whose death has reconciled us to yourself.
Grant that we, who are nourished by his body and blood,
may be filled with his Holy Spirit,
and become one body, one spirit in Christ.

May he make us an everlasting gift to you
and enable us to share in the inheritance of your saints,
with Mary, the virgin mother of God;
with the apostles, the martyrs,
(Saint *N: the saint of the day or the patron saint*) and all your saints,
on whose constant intercession we rely for help.

Lord, may this sacrifice, which has made our peace with you,
advance the peace and salvation of all the world.
Strengthen in faith and love your pilgrim Church on earth;
your servant, Pope *N.*, our bishop *N.*
and all the bishops,
with the clergy and the entire people your Son has gained for you.

Father, hear the prayers of the family you have gathered here before you.
In mercy and love unite all your children
wherever they may be.

Fratres nostros defunctos
et omnes qui, tibi placentes, ex hoc sæculo transierunt,
in regnum tuum benignus admitte,
ubi fore speramus,
ut simul gloria tua perenniter satiemur.
per Christum Dominum nostrum,
per quem mundo bona cuncta largiris.

Or, in Masses for the Dead:

Memento famuli tui (famulæ tuæ) *N.*,
quem (quam) (hodie) ad te ex hoc mundo vocasti.
Concede, ut, qui (quæ) complantatus (complantata)
fuit similitudini mortis Filii tui,
simul fiat et resurrectionis ipsius,
quando mortuos suscitabit in carne de terra
et corpus humilitatis nostræ
configurabit corpori claritatis suæ.
Sed et fratres nostros defunctos,
et omnes qui, tibi placentes, ex hoc sæculo transierunt,
in regnum tuum benignus admitte,
ubi fore speramus,
ut simul gloria tua perenniter satiemur,
quando omnem lacrimam absterges ab oculis nostris,
quia te, sicuti es, Deum nostrum videntes,
tibi similes erimus cuncta per sæcula,
et te sine fine laudabimus,
per Christum Dominum nostrum,
per quem mundo bona cuncta largiris.

---

per ipsum, et cum ipso, et in ipso,
est tibi Deo Patri omnipotenti,
in unitate Spiritus Sancti,
omnis honor et gloria
per omnia sæcula sæculorum.
Amen.

Welcome into your kingdom our departed brothers and sisters
and all who have left this world in your friendship.

We hope to enjoy for ever the vision of your glory,
through Christ our Lord, from whom all good things come.

Or, in Masses for the Dead:

Remember *N.*
In baptism he (she) died with Christ:
may he (she) also share his resurrection,
when Christ will raise our mortal bodies
and make them like his own in glory.
Welcome into your kingdom our departed brothers and sisters,
and all who have left this world in your friendship.
There we hope to share in your glory
when every tear will be wiped away.
On that day we shall see you, our God, as you are
We shall become like you
and praise you for ever through Christ our Lord,
from whom all good things come.

Through him, with him, in him,
in the unity of the Holy Spirit,
all glory and honour is yours,
almighty Father,
for ever and ever.
Amen.

Eucharistic Prayer IV

Confitemur tibi, Pater sancte,
quia magnus es et omnia opera tua
in sapientia et caritate fecisti.
Hominem ad tuam imaginem condidisti,
eique commisisti mundi curam universi,
ut, tibi soli Creatori serviens,
creaturis omnibus imperaret.
Et cum amicitiam tuam, non oboediens, amisisset,
non eum dereliquisti in mortis imperio.
Omnibus enim misericorditer subvenisti,
ut te quærerentes invenirent.
Sed et foedera pluries hominibus obtulisti
eosque per prophetas erudisti in exspectatione salutis.
Et sic, Pater sancte, mundum dilexisti,
ut, completa plenitudine temporum,
Unigenitum tuum nobis mitteres Salvatorem.
Qui, incarnatus de Spiritu Sancto
et natus ex Maria Virgine,
in nostra condicionis forma est conversatus
per omnia absque peccato;
salutem evangelizavit pauperibus,
redemptionem captivis,
mæstis corde lætitiam.
Ut tuam vero dispensationem impleret,
in mortem tradidit semetipsum
ac, resurgens a mortuis,
mortem destruxit vitamque renovavit.
Et, ut non amplius nobismetipsis viveremus,
sed sibi qui pro nobis mortuus est atque surrexit,
a te, Pater, misit Spiritum Sanctum
primitias credentibus,
qui, opus suum in mundo perficiens,
omnem sanctificationem compleret.

Eucharistic Prayer IV

Father, we acknowledge your greatness:
all your actions show your wisdom and love.
You formed man in your own likeness
and set him over the whole world
to serve you, his creator,
and to rule over all creatures.
Even when he disobeyed you and lost your friendship
you did not abandon him to the power of death,
but helped all men to seek and find you.
Again and again you offered a covenant to man,
and through the prophets taught him to hope for
salvation.
Father, you so loved the world
that in the fullness of time you sent your only Son to be
our Saviour.

He was conceived through the power of the Holy Spirit,
and born of the Virgin Mary,
a man like us in all things but sin.
To the poor he proclaimed the good news of salvation,
to prisoners, freedom,
and to those in sorrow, joy.
In fulfilment of your will
he gave himself up to death;
but by rising from the dead,
he destroyed death and restored life.
And that we might live no longer for ourselves but
for him,
he sent the Holy Spirit from you, Father,
as his first gift to those who believe,
to complete his work on earth
and bring us the fullness of grace.

Quæsumus igitur, Domine,
ut idem Spiritus Sanctus
hæc munera sanctificare dignetur,
ut Corpus et ✠ Sanguis fiant
Domini nostri Iesu Christi
ad hoc magnum mysterium celebrandum,
quod ipse nobis reliquit in fœdus æternum.

Ipse enim, cum hora venisset
ut glorificaretur a te, Pater sancte,
ac dilexisset suos qui erant in mundo,
in finem dilexit eos:
et cenantibus illis
accepit panem, benedixit ac fregit,
deditque discipulis suis, dicens:

Accipite et manducate ex hoc omnes:
hoc est enim Corpus meum,
quod pro vobis tradetur.

Simili modo
accipiens calicem, ex genimine vitis repletum,
gratias egit, deditque discipulis suis, dicens:

Accipite et bibite ex eo omnes:
hic est enim calix Sanguinis mei
novi et æterni testamenti,
qui pro vobis et pro multis effundetur
in remissionem peccatorum.

Hoc facite in meam commemorationem.

Father, may this Holy Spirit sanctify these offerings.
Let them become the body ✠ and blood of Jesus Christ
our Lord
as we celebrate the great mystery
which he left us as an everlasting covenant.

He always loved those who were his own in the world.
When the time came for him to be glorified by you,
his heavenly Father,
he showed the depth of his love.
While they were at supper,
he took bread, said the blessing, broke the bread
and gave it to his disciples, saying:

Take this, all of you, and eat it:
this is my body which will be given up for
you.

In the same way, he took the cup, filled with wine.
He gave you thanks, and giving the cup to his disciples,
said:

Take this, all of you, and drink from it:
this is the cup of my blood,
the blood of the new and everlasting covenant.
It will be shed for you and for all men
so that sins may be forgiven.

Do this in memory of me.

C. Mysterium fidei.

The people reply using one of these acclamations:

1. **Mortem tuam annuntiamus, Domine,
et tuam resurrectionem confitemur, donec venias.**

2. **Quotiescumque manducamus panem hunc
et calicem bibimus,
mortem tuam annuntiamus, Domine, donec venias.**

3. **Salvator mundi, salva nos,
qui per crucem et resurrectionem tuam liberasti nos.**

Unde et nos, Domine, redemptionis nostræ memoriale nunc celebrantes,
mortem Christi
eiusque descensum ad inferos recolimus,
eius resurrectionem
et ascensionem ad tuam dexteram profitemur,
et, exspectantes ipsius adventum in gloria,
offerimus tibi eius Corpus et Sanguinem,
sacrificium tibi acceptabile et toti mundo salutare.

Respice, Domine, in Hostiam,
quam Ecclesiæ tuæ ipse parasti,
et concede benignus omnibus
qui ex hoc uno pane participabunt et calice,
ut, in unum corpus a Sancto Spiritu congregati,
in Christo hostia viva perficiantur,
ad laudem gloriæ tuæ.

C. Let us proclaim the mystery of faith :

The people reply using one of these acclamations:

1. **Christ has died,**
   Christ is risen,
   Christ will come again.

2. **Dying you destroyed our death,**
   rising you restored our life.
   Lord Jesus, come in glory.

3. **When we eat this bread and drink this cup,**
   we proclaim your death, Lord Jesus,
   until you come in glory.

4. **Lord, by your cross and resurrection**
   you have set us free.
   You are the Saviour of the world.

Father, we now celebrate this memorial of our redemption.
We recall Christ's death, his descent among the dead,
his resurrection, and his ascension to your right hand ;
and, looking forward to his coming in glory, we offer you his body and blood,
the acceptable sacrifice,
which brings salvation to the whole world.

Lord, look upon this sacrifice which you have given to your Church ;
and by your Holy Spirit, gather all who share this bread and wine*
into the one body of Christ, a living sacrifice of praise.

**or* who share this one bread and one cup

Nunc ergo, Domine, omnium recordare,
pro quibus tibi hanc oblationem offerimus:
in primis famuli tui, Papæ nostri *N.*,
Episcopi nostri *N.*, et Episcoporum ordinis universi,
sed et totius cleri, et offerentium,
et circumstantium,
et cuncti populi tui,
et omnium, qui te quærunt corde sincero.
Memento etiam illorum,
qui obierunt in pace Christi tui,
et omnium defunctorum,
quorum fidem tu solus cognovisti.

Nobis omnibus, filiis tuis, clemens Pater concede,
ut cælestem hereditatem consequi valeamus
cum beata Virgine, Dei Genetrice, Maria,
cum Apostolis et Sanctis tuis
in regno tuo, ubi cum universa creatura,
a corruptione peccati et mortis liberata,
te glorificemus per Christum Dominum nostrum,
per quem mundo bona cuncta largiris.

Per ipsum, et cum ipso, et in ipso,
est tibi Deo Patri omnipotenti,
in unitate Spiritus Sancti,
omnis honor et gloria
per omnia sæcula sæculorum.

P. **Amen.**

Lord, remember those for whom we offer this sacrifice,
especially *N.* our Pope,
N. our bishop, and bishops and clergy everywhere.
Remember those who take part in this offering,
those here present and all your people,
and all who seek you with a sincere heart.
Remember those who have died in the peace of Christ
and all the dead whose faith is known to you alone.

Father, in your mercy grant also to us, your children,
to enter into our heavenly inheritance
in the company of the Virgin Mary, the Mother of God,
and your apostles and saints.
Then, in your kingdom, freed from the corruption of
sin and death,
we shall sing your glory with every creature through
Christ our Lord,
through whom you give us everything that is good.

Through him,
with him,
in him,
in the unit of they Holy Spirit,
all glory and honour is yours,
almighty Father,
for ever and ever.

P. **Amen.**

THE COMMUNION RITE

The celebrant introduces the Lord's Prayer in these or similar words.

C. Præceptis salutaribus moniti,
et divina institutione formati,
audemus dicere:

P. **Pater noster, qui es in cælis:
sanctificetur nomen tuum;
adveniat regnum tuum;
fiat voluntas tua, sicut in cælo, et in terra.
Panem nostrum cotidianum da nobis hodie;
et dimitte nobis debita nostra,
sicut et nos dimittimus debitoribus nostris;
et ne nos inducas in tentationem;
sed libera nos a malo.**

C. Libera nos, quæsumus, Domine, ab omnibus malis,
da propitius pacem in diebus nostris,
ut, ope misericordiæ tuæ adiuti,
et a peccato simus semper liberi
et ab omni perturbatione securi:
exspectantes beatam spem
et adventum Salvatoris nostri Iesu Christi.

P. **Quia tuum est regnum,
et potestas, et gloria
in sæcula.**

C. Domine Iesu Christe, qui dixisti Apostolis tuis:
Pacem relinquo vobis, pacem meam do vobis:
ne respicias peccata nostra,
sed fidem Ecclesiæ tuæ;
eamque secundum voluntatem tuam
pacificare et coadunare digneris.
Qui vivis et regnas in sæcula sæculorum.

P. **Amen.**

THE COMMUNION RITE

The celebrant introduces the Lord's Prayer in these or similar words.

C. Let us pray with confidence to the Father in the words our Saviour gave us:

P. **Our Father, who art in heaven,**
hallowed be thy name.
Thy kingdom come.
Thy will be done on earth, as it is in heaven.
Give us this day our daily bread,
and forgive us our trespasses,
as we forgive those who trespass against us,
and lead us not into temptation,
but deliver us from evil.

C. Deliver us, Lord, from every evil,
and grant us peace in our day.
In your mercy keep us free from sin
and protect us from all anxiety
as we wait in joyful hope
for the coming of our Saviour, Jesus Christ.

P. **For the kingdom, the power, and the glory**
are yours, now and for ever.

C. Lord Jesus Christ, you said to your apostles:
I leave you peace, my peace I give you.
Look not on our sins, but on the faith of your Church,
and grant us the peace and unity of your kingdom
where you live for ever and ever.

P· **Amen.**

C. Pax Domini sit semper vobiscum.

P. **Et cum spiritu tuo.**
C. Offerte vobis pacem.

Agnus Dei, qui tollis peccata mundi: miserere nobis.
Agnus Dei, qui tollis peccata mundi: miserere nobis.
Agnus Dei, qui tollis peccata mundi: dona nobis pacem.

The celebrant says quietly:
Haec commixtio Corporis et Sanguinis Domini nostri Iesu Christi fiat accipientibus nobis in vitam æternam.

He continues in a low voice:
Domine Iesu Christe, Fili Dei vivi,
qui ex voluntate Patris,
cooperante Spiritu Sancto,
per mortem tuam mundum vivificasti:
libera me per hoc sacrosanctum Corpus et Sanguinem tuum
ab omnibus iniquitatibus meis et universis malis:
et fac me tuis semper inhærere mandatis,
et a te numquam separari permittas.

or Perceptio Corporis et Sanguinis tui, Domine Iesu Christe,
non mihl proveniat in iudicium et condemnationem:
sed pro tua pietate prosit mihi ad tutamentum mentis et corporis,
et ad medelam percipiendam.

C. The peace of the Lord be with you always.

P. **And also with you.**
C. Let us offer each other the sign of peace.

Lamb of God, you take away the sins of the world: have mercy on us.
Lamb of God, you take away the sins of the world: have mercy on us.
Lamb of God, you take away the sins of the world: grant us peace.

The celebrant says quietly:
May this mingling of the body and blood of our Lord Jesus Christ
bring eternal life to us who receive it.

He continues in a low voice:
Lord Jesus Christ, Son of the living God,
by the will of the Father and the work of the Holy Spirit
your death brought life to the world.
By your holy body and blood
free me from all my sins and from every evil.
Keep me faithful to your teaching,
and never let me be parted from you.

or Lord Jesus Christ,
with faith in your love and mercy
I eat your body and drink your blood.
Let it not bring me condemnation,
but health in mind and body.

The celebrant genuflects, and raising the host says:
Ecce Agnus Dei, ecce qui tollit peccata mundi.
Beati qui ad cenam Agni vocati sunt.

Domine, non sum dignus, ut intres sub tectum meum:
sed tantum dic verbo, et sanabitur anima mea.

The celebrant says quietly:
Corpus Christi custodiat me in vitam æternam.

He then receives the chalice.
Sanguis Christi custodiat me in vitam æternam.

The communion *of the people follows. A* Communion antiphon *is said or a hymn is sung.*

The celebrant takes a host for each communicant, raises it a little and proclaims:

C. Corpus Christi.

P. **Amen.**

The sign of communion is more complete when given under both kinds and Christ's intention that the new and eternal covenant be ratified in his blood is better expressed. To those receiving the precious blood, the celebrant or deacon says:

C. Sanguis Christi.

P. **Amen.**

The celebrant genuflects and raising the host says.
This is the Lamb of God
who takes away the sins of the world.
Happy are those who are called to his supper.

Lord, I am not worthy to receive you,
but only say the word and I shall be healed.

The celebrant says quietly:
May the body of Christ bring me to everlasting life.

He then receives the chalice.
May the blood of Christ bring me to everlasting life.

The communion *of the people follows. A* Communion antiphon *is said or a hymn is sung.*

The celebrant takes a host for each communicant, raises it a little and proclaims:

C. The body of Christ.

P. **Amen.**

The sign of communion is more complete when given under both kinds and Christ's intention that the new and eternal covenant be ratified in his blood is better expressed. To those receiving the precious blood, the celebrant or deacon says:

C. The blood of Christ.

P. **Amen.**

While cleansing the sacred vessels the celebrant says silently:

Quod ore sumpsimus, Domine, pura mente capiamus, et de munere temporali fiat nobis remedium sempiternum.

Communion over, he may sit in the chair for a time, while all continue to make their thanksgiving.
Then, standing, the celebrant says:

Oremus.

At the end of the prayer:

P. **Amen.**

THE CONCLUDING RITE

C. Dominus vobiscum.

P. **Et cum spiritu tuo.**

C. Benedicat vos omnipotens Deus,
Pater, et Filius, ✠ et Spiritus Sanctus.

P. **Amen.**

C. Ite, missa est.

P. **Deo gratias.**

While cleansing the sacred vessels the celebrant says silently:

Lord, may I receive these gifts in purity of heart.
May they bring me healing and strength, now and for ever.

Communion over, he may sit in the chair for a time, while all continue to make their thanksgiving. Then, standing, the celebrant says:

Let us pray.

At the end of the prayer:

P. **Amen.**

THE CONCLUDING RITE

C. The Lord be with you.

P. **And also with you.**

C. May almighty God bless you,
the Father, and the Son, ✠ and the Holy Spirit.

P. **Amen.**

C. The Mass is ended, go in peace.

P. **Thanks be to God.**

PUBLISHED BY THE INCORPORATED CATHOLIC TRUTH SOCIETY, LONDON
AND PRINTED BY THE BURLEIGH PRESS, FISHPONDS, BRISTOL
Printed in England *July, 1981*